Contents

Key

* easy

** medium

*** difficult

Indian food

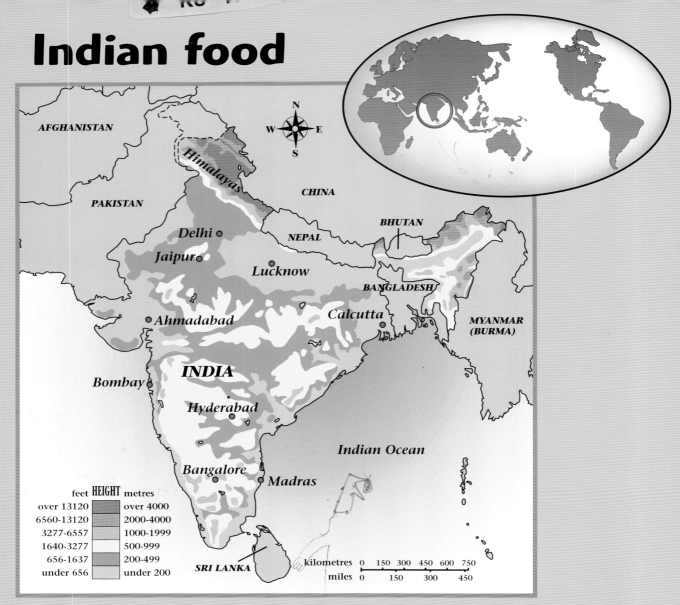

India is a large country in southern Asia. It has a varied climate, with cold mountainous regions in the north and hot, **tropical**, flat areas in the south. Indian cooking is also very varied.

In the past

People have lived on the land that is now India for over five thousand years. The land has been invaded by people from many different countries, who all brought their own cooking traditions with them. During the last 500 years many European countries fought to control India. Much of India was ruled by the British between 1757 and 1947, when India gained its independence.

A World of Recipes

India

Julie McCulloch

Heinemann
LIBRARY

www.heinemann.co.uk
Visit our website to find out more information about **Heinemann Library** books.

To order:
 Phone 44 (0) 1865 888066
Send a fax to 44 (0) 1865 314091
 Visit the Heinemann Bookshop at www.heinemann.co.uk to browse our catalogue and order online.

First published in Great Britain by Heinemann Library, Halley Court, Jordan Hill, Oxford OX2 8EJ, a division of Reed Educational and Professional Publishing Ltd. Heinemann is a registered trademark of Reed Educational & Professional Publishing Limited.

OXFORD MELBOURNE AUCKLAND JOHANNESBURG BLANTYRE
GABORONE IBADAN PORTSMOUTH NH (USA) CHICAGO

© Reed Educational and Professional Publishing Ltd 2002
The moral right of the proprietor has been asserted.

Designed by Tinstar Design (www.tinstar.co.uk)
Illustrations by Nicholas Beresford-Davies
Originated by Dot Gradations
Printed by Wing King Tong in Hong Kong.

CN 641. 5123
500 749660

ISBN 0 431 11703 9   (hardback)
06 05 04 03 02
10 9 8 7 6 5 4 3 2

ISBN 0 431 11710 1   (paperback)
06 05 04 03 02
10 9 8 7 6 5 4 3 2 1

British Library Cataloguing in Publication Data
McCulloch, Julie
    India. – (A world of recipes)
    1. Cookery, India – Juvenile literature 2. India –
    Description and travel – Juvenile literature
    I. Title
    641.5'123'0954

Acknowledgements
The Publishers would like to thank the following for permission to reproduce photographs:
Robert Harding, p.5; All other photographs by Gareth Boden.
Illustration p.45, US Department of Agriculture/US Department of Health and Human Services.

Cover photographs reproduced with permission of Gareth Boden.

Our thanks to Sue Townsend, home economist, and Sue Mildenhall for their comments in the preparation of this book.

Every effort has been made to contact copyright holders of any material reproduced in this book. Any omissions will be rectified in subsequent printings if notice is given to the Publisher.

Words appearing in the text in bold, **like this**, are explained in the glossary.

In India, religion rather than history, has the greatest influence on what people eat. Many Indian people are Hindu. This religion is against any form of violence so many Hindus are **vegetarian**. Some Hindus eat chicken and fish, but eating beef is strictly forbidden, as cows are **sacred** animals. This means that there are lots of vegetarian dishes in Indian cooking.

Around the country

The Himalayas, at the northern border of India, are the highest mountains in the world. In northern India the main crop is wheat, which is ground to make bread. Southern India is very hot and **humid**, and the most important crop is rice. The cooking of southern India is often very spicy.

▲ *The Himalayan mountains are the highest mountains in the world.*

Other crops grown in India include corn, vegetables, bananas, lentils, tea and coffee.

Indian meals

Indian meals usually consist of several small dishes which are all served at the same time. Hot, spicy dishes are balanced by cool, refreshing ones. Rice or bread is normally served with every meal. Several side dishes are usually served, such as raita (see page 36), a salad or pickles. Meals are sometimes finished with a dessert.

Indian people usually eat with their fingers. A piece of bread, or a little rice rolled into a ball, is dipped into a sauce, or used as a scoop.

Ingredients

Labels on image: chapati, naan, ghee, red lentils, coconut milk, rice, turmeric, ginger, garlic, creamed coconut, cumin, garam masala, ground coriander, chilli powder

Bread

Bread is often served as
an accompaniment in India,
and there are many different types. Chapatis are thin
and round and cooked in a hot pan (see page 32).
Naan bread is thick and soft, and cooked in an oven.
Supermarkets often sell ready-made chapatis and naans.

Coconut

Coconut is used in many dishes, especially in southern
India. You may find fresh coconuts in shops, but it is
easier to buy it ready-processed. The recipes in this
book use coconut in three different forms – coconut
milk, which comes in cans; blocks of creamed coconut;
and **desiccated** coconut, which is dried, **grated**, and
sold in packets.

Garlic

Garlic is used in many dishes, especially those from
northern India. You can buy garlic in the vegetable
section of most food shops or supermarkets.

Ginger

Fresh ginger is used in many Indian dishes, usually **peeled** and grated or finely **chopped**. It is readily available in shops and supermarkets. It is better to use fresh rather than dried ginger, as the taste is stronger.

Lentils

Lentils are an important part of many people's diets in India, especially **vegetarians**. They are cheap, and good for you. There are many different types of lentil. The most common type, red lentils, can be found in most shops and supermarkets.

Oil

Most savoury Indian dishes are cooked in ghee. Ghee is a type of purified butter. It gives a rich, buttery taste to Indian food. Ghee can be difficult to find, so the recipes in this book use vegetable oil or corn oil.

Rice

Rice is an important ingredient in Indian cooking. It comes in two main types – short grain and long grain. Long grain rice (especially an Indian rice called basmati) is more suitable for most Indian dishes.

Spices

Spices are plants or seeds with strong flavours, which are used to add taste. They are an essential ingredient in many Indian dishes. Some of the most common spices are cumin, turmeric, coriander, garam masala and chilli powder (see page 11 for more about coriander and page 27 for garam masala). You only need to use small amounts of spices. Chilli powder is very hot, so you may prefer to use less, or leave it out if you don't like food that is too spicy. All of these spices can easily be bought dried in jars or boxes.

Before you start

Kitchen rules

There are a few basic rules you should always follow when you are cooking.

- Ask an adult if you can use the kitchen.
- Some cooking processes, especially those involving hot water or oil, can be dangerous. When you see this sign, take extra care or ask an adult to help.
- Wash your hands before you start.
- Wear an apron to protect your clothes, and tie back long hair.
- Be very careful when you use sharp knives.
- Never leave pan handles sticking out in case you knock them.
- Always wear oven gloves to lift things in and out of the oven.
- Wash fruit and vegetables before you use them.

How long will it take?

Some of the recipes in this book are quick and easy, and some are more difficult and take longer. The strip across the top of the right hand page of each recipe tells you how long it takes to cook each dish from start to finish. It also shows how difficult each dish is to make: every recipe is either * (easy), ** (medium) or *** (difficult).

Quantities and measurements

You can see how many people each recipe will serve at the top of the right hand page, too. Most of the recipes in this book make enough to feed two people. Where it is more sensible to make a larger amount, though, the recipes makes enough for four. You can multiply or divide the quantities if you want to cook for more or fewer people.

Ingredients for recipes can be measured in two ways. Metric measurements use grams and millilitres. Imperial measurements use ounces and fluid ounces. This book uses metric measurements. If you want to convert these into imperial measurements, see the chart on page 44.

In the recipes you will see the following abbreviations:

tbsp = tablespoon   g = grams
tsp = teaspoon   ml = millilitres

Utensils

To cook the recipes in this book, you will need these utensils (as well as kitchen essentials such as spoons, plates and bowls):

- chopping board
- colander or sieve
- fish slice
- food processor or blender
- frying pan
- grater
- measuring jug
- rolling pin
- saucepan with lid
- set of scales
- sharp knife

(!) Whenever you use kitchen knives, be very careful.

Butter beans with sultanas

Beans are used in many Indian dishes, and are a very good source of **protein**. This simple bean dish could be served as a starter or as an accompaniment to a main course.

What you need

1 tbsp fresh coriander leaves (see page 11)
1 tbsp oil
400g canned butter beans
¼ tsp turmeric (see page 19)
¼ tsp chilli powder (optional)
2 tbsp sultanas
1 tsp sugar
1 tbsp lemon juice

What you do

1 Finely **chop** the coriander.

2 **Drain** the liquid from the butter beans by emptying them into a sieve or colander.

3 Heat the oil in a frying pan over a medium heat.

4 Add the butter beans, and cook for 1 minute.

5 Turn the heat down to low. Add the turmeric, chilli powder (if using), sultanas, sugar and lemon juice. Cook for a further 5 minutes.

6 Add 2 tbsp water and **simmer** for 5 minutes.

7 Sprinkle the chopped coriander over the beans and sultanas before serving.

CORIANDER

Coriander is used in two forms in Indian food – fresh coriander leaves (a herb) and ground coriander (a spice). Coriander leaves have a strong, fresh taste. They are used for their flavour, to add decoration and for the bright green colour they give to sauces. You need about as many leaves as will fit in a tablespoon for the recipes in this book.

Ground coriander is made from the crushed seeds of the coriander plant. Ground coriander is added to many Indian dishes, and adds a strong, slightly lemony taste.

11

Fish and coconut soup

Savoury Indian dishes are not traditionally divided into starters or main courses. Several small dishes are usually all served at the same time. This soup would be just one of them.

This recipe suggests using cod, but you could use any sort of white fish. Try to find fish fillets without the skin on. If you use frozen fish, take it out of the freezer and put it into the fridge at least 12 hours before using it, so that it is completely **thawed**.

What you need

½ onion
1 clove garlic
small piece fresh ginger
   (about 2cm long)
2 skinless cod fillets
1 tbsp oil
1 tsp turmeric (see page 19)
¼ tsp chilli powder (optional)
400ml coconut milk
1 tbsp lemon juice

What you do

1 **Peel** the skin from the onion, and finely **chop** it.

2 Peel the skin from the garlic clove and ginger, and finely chop them.

3 Cut the cod fillets into small pieces.

(!) 4 Heat the oil in a saucepan over a medium heat. Add the chopped onion, garlic, ginger, turmeric and chilli powder (if using), and **fry** for 5 minutes.

5 Add the coconut milk, and bring the mixture to the **boil**.

6 Add the fish pieces and lemon juice. Turn the heat down to medium, and **simmer** the soup for 10 minutes.

Spicy scrambled eggs

The Parsi people, who live in western India, originally came from the land that is now Iran. When they arrived in India, they brought with them many egg dishes, like this recipe for scrambled eggs. In India, this dish could be eaten for breakfast, tea or supper.

What you need

small piece fresh ginger
(about 2cm long)
1 clove garlic
½ onion
1 tbsp fresh coriander
leaves (see page 11)
3 eggs
1 tbsp oil
¼ tsp chilli powder
(optional)
¼ tsp turmeric (see page 19)

What you do

1 **Peel** the skin from the ginger and garlic, and finely **chop** them.

2 Peel the skin from the onion, and finely chop it.

3 Finely chop the coriander leaves.

4 Crack the eggs into a small bowl. **Beat** them with a fork or a whisk until the yolk and the white are mixed.

5 Heat the oil in a saucepan over a medium heat. Add the chopped ginger, garlic, onion, chilli powder (if using) and turmeric, and **fry** for 5 minutes.

6 Add the beaten eggs and chopped coriander. Cook for 5 minutes, stirring often with a wooden spoon, until the eggs start to become solid. Serve immediately.

Chicken bhuna

'Bhuna', which can also be spelled 'bhoona', means **fried**. Bhuna dishes are made from fried onions and spices. When coconut is added to this mixture, it makes a rich, creamy sauce.

What you need

2 chicken breasts
1 onion
1 clove garlic
3 tomatoes
1 tbsp oil
½ tsp garam masala
   (see page 27)
½ tsp ground coriander
   (see page 11)
¼ tsp chilli powder (optional)
½ tsp turmeric (see page 19)
25g creamed coconut

What you do

1 Cut the chicken breasts into bite-sized pieces.

2 **Peel** the skin from the onion and garlic, and finely **chop** them.

3 Chop the tomatoes into small pieces.

4 Heat the oil in a saucepan over a medium heat. Add the chopped onion, garlic, garam masala, coriander, chilli powder (if using) and turmeric. Fry for 5 minutes.

5 Add the chicken pieces and chopped tomatoes. Cook the mixture for 20 minutes.

6 While the bhuna is cooking, cut the creamed coconut into small pieces. Stir the coconut into the bhuna. Serve this dish with plain, boiled rice.

PLAIN BOILED RICE

This recipe makes enough plain boiled rice for 2 people:

1 Put 140g rice into a saucepan.

2 Add 400ml water

3 Bring to the boil, then **simmer** for 20 minutes, stirring occasionally, until the rice has soaked up all the water.

Prawn patia

'Patia' is a sweet and sour dish – the honey gives the sweet taste, and the vinegar the sourness. Serve with plain boiled rice (see recipe on page 17), or with the pilau rice recipe (see page 30).

What you need

½ onion
1 clove garlic
small piece fresh
  ginger (about 2cm
  long)
1 tbsp oil
½ tsp cumin
½ tsp turmeric
½ tsp ground
  coriander
1 tsp paprika
2 tbsp natural yoghurt
1 tbsp honey
2 tsp vinegar
300g cooked peeled
  prawns
1 tbsp fresh coriander
  leaves (see page 11)

What you do

1 **Peel** the skin from the onion, and finely **chop** it.

2 Peel the skin from the garlic and ginger, and finely chop them.

(!) **3** Heat the oil in a saucepan over a medium heat. Add the chopped onion, garlic, ginger, cumin, turmeric, ground coriander and paprika, and **fry** for 5 minutes.

4 Reduce the heat, add the yoghurt, honey and vinegar, and **simmer** for 5 minutes.

5 Add the prawns, and simmer the mixture for a further 5 minutes.

6 Finely chop the fresh coriander leaves and sprinkle them over your patia.

TURMERIC AND SAFFRON

Turmeric is a spice used in many Indian dishes to give a distinctive taste and a bright yellow colour. It is sometimes used as a substitute for saffron, another spice which colours food yellow. Saffron is made from the centre of crocus flowers, and is very expensive.

Banana curry

This fruity curry (see page 21) has a sweet, spicy taste. It is best to use unripe bananas, which are still slightly green, to make this dish.

What you need

small piece fresh ginger
  (about 2cm long)
2 bananas
1 tbsp oil
½ tsp garam masala
  (see page 27)
½ tsp cumin
¼ tsp chilli powder
  (optional)
½ tsp turmeric
  (see page 19)
200ml natural yoghurt
1 tbsp lemon juice

What you do

1 **Peel** the skin from the ginger, and finely **chop** it.

2 Peel the bananas, and cut them into **slices** about 1cm thick.

(!) **3** Heat the oil in a saucepan over a medium heat. Add the chopped ginger, garam masala, cumin, chilli powder (if using) and turmeric, and **fry** for about 3 minutes.

4 Add the pieces of banana, and stir them into the spices until they are well coated.

5 Reduce the heat and add the yoghurt and lemon juice. **Simmer** the curry for 10 minutes.

WHAT IS A CURRY?

The word 'curry' is used to describe any spicy Indian dish. Indian people don't use it, and no one knows for sure where the word came from. One theory is that 'curry' may have come from the Indian word 'karahi', which is a type of frying pan used all over India for cooking spices.

Spicy chick peas

This is a very filling **vegetarian** dish. Like beans and lentils, chick peas are an important source of **protein**. You could eat this dish the Indian way, by tearing off pieces of chapati (see page 32) and using them to scoop up the chick peas.

What you need

1 clove garlic
1 onion
2 tomatoes
125g canned chick peas
¼ tsp chilli powder (optional)
1 tbsp oil
½ tsp ground coriander (see page 11)
½ tsp garam masala (see page 27)
½ tsp turmeric (see page 19)
1 tbsp lemon juice

What you do

1 **Peel** the skin from the garlic and onion, and finely **chop** them.

2 Chop the tomatoes into small pieces.

3 **Drain** the liquid from the chick peas by emptying the can into a colander or sieve.

4 Heat the oil in a saucepan over a medium heat. Add the chopped garlic, onion, chilli powder (if using), coriander, garam masala and turmeric, and **fry** for 5 minutes.

5 Add the chopped tomatoes, drained chick peas and lemon juice. Cook for 10 minutes.

LUCKY CHICK PEAS

Chick peas are known as 'channa' in India. Many Hindus eat channa on Fridays, because they believe this will bring them luck.

Vegetable biryani

A 'biryani' is a dish made of rice with other ingredients added to it. It makes a filling main course.

What you need

½ onion
1 clove garlic
½ carrot
1 courgette
1 vegetable stock cube
1 tbsp oil
1 tsp ground cinnamon
½ tsp turmeric (see page 19)
½ tsp garam masala (see page 27)
100g rice
60g fresh or frozen peas
60g chopped, mixed nuts
25g sultanas

What you do

1 Peel the skin from the onion and garlic, and finely **chop** them.

2 Wash the carrot, then cut it into small pieces.

3 Cut off the top and bottom of the courgette, then **slice** one half of it. Cut each slice into four.

4 Put 450ml water into a saucepan, and bring it to the **boil**. Crumble the stock cube into the water, and stir until it **dissolves**. Put the stock to one side.

5 Heat the oil in a saucepan over a medium heat. Add the chopped onion, garlic, cinnamon, turmeric and garam masala, and **fry** for about 3 minutes.

6 Add the rice, and fry for a further 5 minutes, stirring occasionally.

7 Add the chopped carrot, courgette, frozen peas and vegetable stock. Stir well, then reduce the heat to low and **cover** the pan.

8 **Simmer** the mixture for about 20 minutes, stirring from time to time, until all the liquid has been soaked up and the rice is soft.

9 Stir in the chopped nuts and sultanas, then serve.

MORE BIRYANIS

There are many different variations on the basic biryani. You could make a meat biryani by adding some chopped-up cooked chicken, or a fish biryani by adding cooked prawns or fish.

Spicy okra

Okra is a vegetable which grows in many parts of India. It is also known as 'bindi' or 'ladies' fingers'. Okra does not have a very strong flavour, but is excellent at picking up the taste of spices in a dish. When you cook okra, you will see that it produces lots of sticky 'threads'. This is perfectly normal! If you can't find okra, try making this dish with aubergine instead. Chop an aubergine into 1cm cubes, then cook it in the same way as the okra.

What you need

1 onion
2 cloves garlic
2 tomatoes
250g okra
1 tbsp oil
1 tsp ground coriander (see page 11)
½ tsp turmeric (see page 19)
1 tsp garam masala (see page 27)

What you do

1 **Peel** the skin from the onion and garlic, and finely **chop** them.

2 Chop the tomatoes into pieces.

3 Cut the tops and bottoms off the okra, then cut the okra into 1cm **slices**.

⚠ **4** Heat the oil in a saucepan over a medium heat. Add the chopped onion, garlic, coriander, turmeric and garam masala, and **fry** for 5 minutes.

5 Reduce the heat, add the okra slices and chopped tomatoes. **Simmer** the mixture for 10 minutes.

GARAM MASALA

'Garam masala' means 'hot mixture'. It is a mixture of spices that is added to many Indian dishes to add flavour. You can buy ready-mixed garam masala in jars or boxes, but most Indian cooks make their own. It is made by **toasting** black peppercorns, cinnamon, cloves, coriander and cumin in a frying pan without oil, then **grinding** the toasted spices into a fine powder.

Lentil patties

Over 60 varieties of lentils are grown in India. The most common are red lentils, although other types of lentils could also be used in this dish. Check on the packet to see if they need soaking first.

What you need

2 spring onions
1 tbsp fresh coriander leaves (see page 11)
125g lentils
¼ tsp chilli powder (optional)
½ tsp turmeric (see page 19)
3 tbsp plain flour
2 tbsp oil

What you do

1 Cut the tops and bottoms off the spring onions, and finely **chop** them.

2 Finely chop the coriander leaves.

3 Put the lentils into a saucepan with 200ml water. Bring the water to the **boil**, then reduce the heat. **Cover** the pan and **simmer** the lentils for about 20 minutes, until the lentils have soaked up all the water.

4 Add the chopped spring onions, coriander, chilli powder (if using), turmeric and flour. Mix everything together well.

5 Divide the lentil mixture into six pieces. Rub a bit of oil into your hands so that the mixture does not stick, then form each piece into a ball. Squash each ball to flatten it into a patty.

! **6** Heat the rest of the oil in a non-stick frying pan over a medium heat. Carefully put the lentil patties into the pan.

7 Cook the patties on one side for 10 minutes, then turn them over using a fish slice and cook them on the other side for another 10 minutes.

Pilau rice with fruit and nuts

This rice dish can be a main course or a side dish. The fruits and nuts are very good at balancing the spiciness of dishes such as spicy okra (see page 26), prawn patia (see page 18) or chicken bhuna (see page 16).

What you need

1 vegetable stock cube
1 onion
1 tbsp oil
1 tsp ground coriander (see page 11)
½ tsp ground cumin
2 tbsp sultanas
50g canned pineapple chunks or 2 chopped slices
2 tbsp cashew nuts
140g rice

What you do

1 Put 400ml water into a pan, and bring it to the **boil**. Crumble the stock cube into the water, and stir until it **dissolves**. Put the stock to one side.

2 Peel the skin from the onion and finely **chop** half of it.

3 Heat the oil in a saucepan over a medium heat. Add the chopped onion, coriander and cumin, and **fry** for 5 minutes.

4 Add the sultanas and pineapple and fry for a further 5 minutes.

5 Add the cashew nuts, vegetable stock and rice, and bring the mixture to the boil.

6 Reduce the heat to low. **Cover** the pan and **simmer** for about 20 minutes, stirring occasionally to stop the rice from sticking to the pan, until all the liquid has been soaked up and the rice is soft.

CASHEW NUTS

Cashew trees are common in India. Their nuts, known as cashew nuts, are used in lots of Indian dishes. They can be added whole, as in this dish, or ground up to make a type of flour, which is used to thicken sauces.

Chapatis

Chapatis are soft, flat circles of bread. They are eaten with many different Indian dishes, and are often used as a scoop to pick up food.

What you need

140g plain flour
½ tsp salt

What you do

1 Put the salt and 125g of the flour into a bowl.

2 Gradually stir in 100ml water. Mix well until the mixture forms a dough.

3 Sprinkle the rest of the flour onto a worktop. Turn the dough out of the bowl, and **knead** it for about 10 minutes, until it is smooth.

4 Divide the dough into six pieces. Using a rolling pin, roll out each piece of dough into a thin circle.

5 Heat a non-stick frying pan over a medium heat, without adding any oil. Put one chapati into the pan.

6 Cook the chapati for about 1 minute, until it has brown patches. Turn it over using a fish slice and cook the other side for a further minute.

7 Cook the rest of the chapatis in the same way.

INDIAN BREADS

Bread is very popular in India. It can be **baked**, fried or **grilled**. In many cities you can find bread sellers called 'tandoor wallahs'. They set up portable ovens called 'tandoors' on street corners, and use them to cook bread for the nearby households.

Corn and coconut salad

This salad is an ideal accompaniment to a spicy main course. It is quick and easy to make, too.

What you need

100g frozen sweetcorn
1 tbsp fresh coriander
   leaves (see page 11)
50g **desiccated**
   coconut
2 tbsp lemon juice
¼ tsp chilli powder
   (optional)

What you do

1 Put the sweetcorn into a saucepan. Add enough water to cover it.

2 Bring to the **boil**, then reduce the heat to a **simmer**. Simmer the sweetcorn for 5 minutes.

3 **Drain** the water from the sweetcorn by emptying the pan into a sieve or colander.

4 Run cold water over the sweetcorn to cool it, then put it into a salad bowl.

5 **Chop** the coriander leaves, then add them to the salad bowl.

6 Add the desiccated coconut, lemon juice and chilli powder (if using) to the salad bowl.

7 Mix everything together well, then serve.

CORN

Corn is grown all over India. The grains of the corn are often used as a vegetable, as in this dish. They can also be ground into a type of flour, which is used to make bread and thicken sauces.

Raita

Because many Indian dishes are quite spicy, they are often accompanied by light, fresh dishes such as raita. The main ingredient in raita is yoghurt, which can be mixed with other ingredients, such as vegetables and herbs.

What you need

100ml plain yoghurt
1 tbsp fresh coriander leaves (see page 11)
¼ tsp nutmeg

What you do

1 Put the yoghurt into a small bowl.

2 Finely **chop** the coriander, and add it to the yoghurt.

3 Add the nutmeg.

4 Mix everything together, then serve.

Sultana raita

Mixed raita

Plain raita

Mint raita

Potato raita

MORE RAITA RECIPES

There are many different variations to the basic raita.
You may like to try some of them.

Mixed raita

Chop a 3cm long piece of cucumber, ½ onion and a tomato
into small pieces. Add them to the basic raita.

Sultana raita

Add 1 tbsp sultanas to the basic raita.

Mint raita

Finely chop 1 tbsp fresh mint leaves.
Add them to the basic raita.

Potato raita

Wash a medium potato, then chop it into small pieces.
Boil the potato pieces in enough water to cover them for
5 minutes. **Drain** the potatoes, then add them to
the basic raita.

Banana fritters

The bananas and sugar in this dish make an ideal change of taste from the spicy, savoury Indian main courses.

What you need

2 eggs
1 tbsp sugar
2 tbsp plain flour
150ml milk
3 bananas
1 tbsp oil

What you do

1 Crack the eggs into a large bowl. **Beat** them with a fork or a whisk until the yolk and the white are mixed.

2 Add the sugar, flour and milk. Mix everything together well.

3 **Peel** the bananas, and cut them into **slices**. Add them to the bowl.

4 Heat the oil in a frying pan over a medium heat. Carefully spoon all the banana fritter mixture into the frying pan.

5 Gently **fry** the fritter for 5 minutes, then turn it over with a fish slice and cook the other side for a further 5 minutes.

6 Slide the fritter onto a plate, and cut it into four portions.

EXPENSIVE DECORATION

Indian desserts are sometimes decorated with tissue-thin
sheets of real silver called 'varaq'. The silver may be wrapped
around nuts which are then placed on top of the food, or
simply draped over the dish. On very special occasions, pure
gold may be used instead!

Kulfi

Kulfi is a type of Indian ice cream. It makes a creamy, cooling end to a meal. People have made ice cream in India for centuries. There is an Indian legend that the emperors sent runners up into the Himalayan mountains to fetch huge chunks of ice to make ice cream. But by the time the runner arrived back at the palace, the ice had always melted!

Take the kulfi out of the freezer at least half an hour before you want to eat it, to give it time to soften.

What you need

25g shelled, unsalted
   pistachio nuts
100g evaporated milk
200ml double cream
25g sugar
1 tsp vanilla essence

What you do

1 **Chop** the pistachio nuts into tiny pieces using a sharp knife.

2 Put the evaporated milk and cream into a saucepan. Bring them to the **boil**.

3 Add the sugar and vanilla essence, then reduce the heat to low.

4 **Simmer** the mixture for 15 minutes, stirring often. The mixture will gradually get thicker.

5 Empty the mixture into a bowl, add the chopped pistachio nuts, and leave to cool.

6 When the mixture is cold, put the bowl in the freezer.

7 You need to leave the kulfi to freeze for at least 5 hours before serving it.

KULFI MOULDS

In India, kulfi is usually frozen in small, metal, cone-shaped moulds to give it a distinctive shape.

Lassi

Lassi is a traditional Indian drink, which is served as an accompaniment to a meal. Lassi comes in both savoury and sweet versions. The savoury version is called 'lassi namkeen', and the sweet version is called 'lassi meethi'.

What you need

Savoury lassi:
6 ice cubes
150ml plain yoghurt
150ml milk
¼ tsp ground cumin

Sweet lassi:
6 ice cubes
1 mango
150ml plain yoghurt
150ml milk
2 tsp sugar

What you do

Savoury lassi

1 Wrap the ice cubes in a tea towel and crush them with a rolling pin.

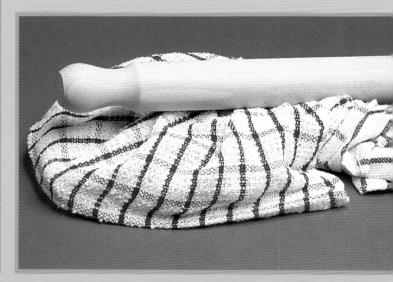

2 Put all the other ingredients into a blender or food processor.

3 **Blend** everything together on the highest setting.

4 Put the crushed ice into two glasses.

5 Pour the lassi over the ice, into the glasses.

Sweet lassi

1 Wrap the ice cubes in a tea towel and crush them with a rolling pin.

2 **Peel** the mango and remove the stone from the middle.

3 Cut the mango into pieces.

4 Put the mango pieces, yoghurt, milk and sugar into a blender or food processor.

5 Blend everything together on the highest setting.

6 Put the crushed ice into two glasses.

7 Pour the lassi over the ice, into the glasses.

BUTTERMILK

Another popular drink in India is buttermilk. Buttermilk is the milky liquid that is left when cream is made into butter. In India, buttermilk is often drunk with breakfast or lunch. If you can find it in the shops, try it and see what you think.

43

Further information

Here are some places to find out more about India and Indian cooking.

Books

A Taste of India
Roz Denny, Raintree Steck-Vaughn, 1994
Cooking the Indian way
Vijay Madavan, Lerner, 1985
World Focus: India
Amanda Barker, Heinemann Library, 1996

Websites

soar.berkeley.edu/recipes/ethnic/indian
www.astray.com/recipes/?search=indian
www.bitesofasia.com/home.html
www.incore.com/india/cuisine.html
www.yumyum.com/recipes.htm

Conversion chart

Ingredients for recipes can be measured in two different ways. Metric measurements use grams and millilitres. Imperial measurements use ounces and fluid ounces. This book uses metric measurements. The chart here shows you how to convert measurements from metric to imperial.

SOLIDS		LIQUIDS	
METRIC	IMPERIAL	METRIC	IMPERIAL
10g	¼ oz	30ml	1 fl oz
15g	½ oz	50ml	2 fl oz
25g	1 oz	75ml	2½ fl oz
50g	1¾ oz	100ml	3½ fl oz
75g	2¾ oz	125ml	4 fl oz
100g	3½ oz	150ml	5 fl oz
150g	5 oz	300ml	10 fl oz
250g	9 oz	600ml	20 fl oz

Healthy eating

This diagram shows which foods you should eat to stay healthy. Most of your food should come from the bottom of the pyramid. Eat some of the foods from the middle every day. Only eat a little of the foods from the top.

Healthy eating, Indian style

In India, most meals include rice, chapatis or naan bread, which all belong to the bottom layer of this pyramid. Some people eat some chicken and fish, but many people are **vegetarian**, and eat beans and lentils instead. With spicy vegetable dishes, and cooling salads you can see how healthy Indian cooking is!

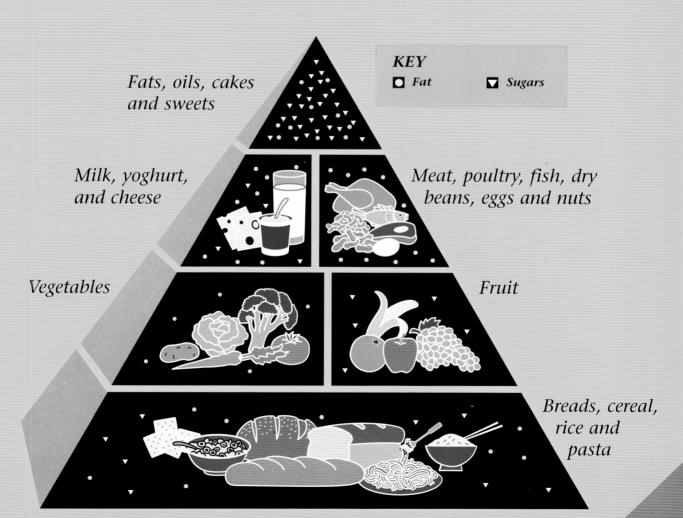

Fats, oils, cakes and sweets

KEY
◻ Fat   ▽ Sugars

Milk, yoghurt, and cheese

Meat, poultry, fish, dry beans, eggs and nuts

Vegetables

Fruit

Breads, cereal, rice and pasta

Glossary

bake cook something in the oven

beat mix something together strongly, such as egg yolks and whites

blend mix ingredients together in a blender or food processor

boil cook a liquid on the hob. Boiling liquid bubbles and steams strongly.

chop cut something into pieces using a knife

cover put a lid on a pan, or foil over a dish

desiccated desiccated coconut is coconut which has had most of the moisture removed from it

dissolve mix something, such as sugar, until it disappears into a liquid

drain remove liquid, usually by pouring into a sieve or colander

fry cook something in oil in a pan

grate break something, such as cheese, into small pieces using a grater

grill cook something under the grill

grind crush something, such as the seed of a spice plant, until it is a powder

humid a climate that is hot and wet

knead mix ingredients into a smooth dough, such as that for bread. Kneading involves pushing with your hands to make the dough smooth.

peel remove the skin of a fruit or vegetable

protein an essential part of a healthy diet. Protein can be found in food such as meat, beans and lentils. Because many Indian people are vegetarian, they eat lots of beans and lentils to make sure they get enough protein.

sacred holy, or respected because of religious laws

simmer cook a liquid on the hob. Simmering liquid bubbles and steams gently.

slice cut something into thin, flat pieces

thaw defrost something which has been frozen

toast in this book, cook something in a pan without any oil in it

tropical a hot, wet climate

vegetarian food that does not contain any meat or fish. People who don't eat meat are called vegetarians.

Index